Oxford Primary History

Mrs Pankhurst

A famous suffragette

Tim Vicary

Oxford University Press 1993

Has your school ever been closed for voting?
Every four or five years, people choose a new government.

They put a piece of paper in a box to say who they want.
These pieces of paper are called 'votes.'
Nowadays every grown-up can vote.

When Mrs Pankhurst grew up, no women could vote.
Only men could vote.
'That's not fair,' she said. 'Why can't women vote too?'

Mrs Pankhurst tried to help poor women.
Some mothers worked twelve hours a day, for ten or twelve pence.
Their children had dirty clothes and no shoes.
Mrs Pankhurst was angry about this. She wanted to help them.

Mrs Pankhurst had two daughters, Christabel and Sylvia.
They went to a meeting with their friend, Annie.
Important men were saying 'Vote for us.'

‘Will you give votes to women?’ Christabel asked.
None of the men said they would.
Christabel and Annie asked their question again.
They were pushed outside, and sent to prison.

Annie and Sylvia came out of prison. They chalked messages on the pavement, to call women to meetings.

Then they hired a big hall. Thousands of women came.
Mrs Pankhurst spoke to them.
'Men are not fair to women,' she said.
'They treat us like children. We work hard but we have no money.
Nothing will get better until they let us vote.'

The women marched to Parliament.
'Votes for Women!' they shouted.
People in the street watched them
and laughed.

'I want to talk to the Prime Minister,'
Mrs Pankhurst said.
'You can't!' the police said.
They pushed her away.
Some women chained themselves to railings.

'We won't go until we can see the Prime Minister!' they said.
The policemen cut the chains, and took the women to prison.

There was a big meeting in Hyde Park in London.
The women wore purple, white and green.
Half a million people came. Mrs Pankhurst spoke to them.
'We will win in the end,' she said. 'Women will change the world!'

There were things for sale, and talks as well.
Lots of women came to learn, and help.

Mrs Pankhurst decided to trick the police.
'We're having a big meeting tomorrow,' she told them.
The police were ready and waiting outside Parliament.

But the women went to the middle of London instead.
They took hammers out of their bags, and smashed shop windows.
Mrs Pankhurst was arrested by the police.

All the people in the court were men.
'We don't want to break things,' Mrs Pankhurst told them.
'We just want you to be fair.

You all have mothers and wives and daughters.
If you love them, why don't you give them the vote?'
Some men supported her, but the judge sent her to prison, just the same.

‘I’m not staying here!’ Mrs Pankhurst said.
‘I won’t eat until you let me out!’

When Sylvia was in prison, they held her,
and a doctor put a tube down her throat.
Then they poured soup down it.
When they stopped she was sick, but she still wouldn't eat.
At last, Mrs Pankhurst and Sylvia were let out.

'We'll ask the King to help,' Mrs Pankhurst said. She marched to Buckingham Palace, but she was arrested again.

She still wouldn't eat or drink in prison.
'Mrs Pankhurst will die!' the women said.
'Please stop it! Please! Give us the vote!'
But the Government still didn't listen.

The First World War began, and women were let out of prison.
'We must help win the war,' Mrs Pankhurst said.
Women worked hard in factories and farms.
After the war, women were at last given the vote.

Today, we have women in government.
Mrs Thatcher was a woman Prime Minister.
These changes all started with Mrs Pankhurst.

Timeline for Mrs Pankhurst

July 1853	Mrs Pankhurst is born.
1893	Mrs Pankhurst works to help the poor.
October 1905	Christabel and Annie are thrown out of the meeting. Christabel is sent to prison for a week, Annie for 3 days.
February 1906	Mrs Pankhurst speaks to a big meeting in London.
January 1908	Women chain themselves to railings.
June 1908	There is a big meeting in Hyde Park.
March 1912	Windows are smashed in London's West End.
May 1912	Mrs Pankhurst is sentenced to 9 months in prison, (but she's let out when she won't eat).
April 1913	Mrs Pankhurst is sentenced to 3 years in prison, (but she's let out when she won't eat).
May 1914	Mrs Pankhurst is arrested outside Buckingham Palace.
August 1914	War with Germany begins.
January 1918	Women over 30 are allowed to vote.
June 1928	All adult women can vote.

Oxford University Press, Walton Street, Oxford OX2 6DP

Oxford New York Toronto
Delhi Bombay Calcutta Madras Karachi
Kuala Lumpur Singapore Hong Kong Tokyo
Nairobi Dar es Salaam Cape Town
Melbourne Auckland Madrid

and associated companies in
Berlin Ibadan

Oxford is a trade mark of Oxford University Press

Illustrations by Chris Molan

0 19 917233 1
0 19 917243 9 (pack of 6)

Typeset by Pentacor PLC, High Wycombe, Bucks
Printed in Hong Kong